noodles

noodles

VICKI LILEY

PERIPLUS
EDITIONS

contents

noodles

Noodles have been eaten by the Chinese for many hundreds of years. Originally, wheat was the main food supply of northern China and was ground to a flour and mixed with water to form a dough. From this dough the Chinese made noodles, steamed bread and celestial pancakes. They also discovered that by mixing eggs into the dough they could make egg noodles, and by rolling the dough out and cutting it into shapes they could use the shapes to enclose fillings of meat and vegetables, which were then steamed or fried. Rice became a staple food in many other parts of Asia. Ground rice flour was mixed with water to form a dough that was used to make rice stick noodles, rice vermicelli and spring roll wrappers.

According to the history books, when Marco Polo visited China in the thirteenth century, he was intrigued by the food the Chinese were constantly consuming, especially the noodles. On his return to Europe he introduced the Chinese staple to Europe. Absorbed into the existing cuisine, round noodles became known as spaghetti; thin noodles as vermicelli; wontons as ravioli; and egg rolls and spring rolls as cannelloni.

Noodles are now eaten worldwide and are available in every shape and size. Once made only by hand, noodles are now mass-produced. In some noodle bars in Shanghai, Hong Kong and Singapore, you can still see the chef make noodles at your table. A piece of fresh dough is manipulated by swinging it from hand to hand until it reaches a length of approximately 6 feet (2 meters). This process requires great skill and practice and is breathtaking to watch.

Many local markets in the West carry a supply of Chinese and Japanese noodles, as well as Asian vegetables and seasonings. This book offers recipes that combine Asian and Western ingredients, using quick-cooking methods—from soups and salads to dishes with meat, poultry, and seafood, to desserts. All of them allow you to enjoy the ancient food of Asia: the noodle.

Cellophane (bean thread) noodles

A thin translucent dried noodle, made from the starch of mung beans and sold in bundles. This noodle has little or no taste. Once softened in hot water, it becomes gelatinous and slippery, hence its alternate names, "bean threads" and "bean shreds." Cellophane noodles are delicious deep-fried, used in fillings for a crisp texture or made in to crunchy nests for stir-fries. Softened in hot water, they can be added to soups, laksas, stir-fries and fillings. Cellophane noodles are difficult to cut or separate when dried, so it is best to buy them in small bundles if possible. Use thin rice vermicelli or angel hair pasta if unavailable.

Egg noodles

Available in a variety of widths—thin, round or flat—and sold fresh and dried in Asian markets. Used extensively in all Asian cooking, egg noodles do not stick together when stir-fried. They make a satisfying meal and absorb dressings when used in salads. They are also delicious deep-fried. Substitute fresh or dried spaghetti if unavailable.

CELLOPHANE NOODLES

EGG NOODLES

Hokkien noodles

These popular thick, round yellow noodles are readily available fresh in the refrigerator cases of most supermarkets. Generally made from wheat flour, egg and water, they are traditionally used in Chinese stir-fries and soups. If unavailable, dried egg noodles or fresh or dried pasta can be substituted. Hokkien noodles keep in the refrigerator for up to seven days.

HOKKIEN NOODLES

Ramen noodles

Ramen noodles are well known for their use in Japanese instant soup. These wiggly noodles are usually sold dried in brightly colored packages. Made from egg dough, they are traditionally used in soups and broths. Substitute thin egg noodles or thin spaghetti if unavailable.

RAMEN NOODLES

RICE STICK NOODLES

Rice stick noodles

Made from ground rice and water, rice stick noodles are widely available dried or fresh in a vast variety of sizes and textures. Rice vermicelli, thin rice stick noodles, are used in soups and are deep-fried for fillings, nests and garnishes. Medium rice stick noodles are added to soups, stir-fries and salads, and the larger variety is suitable in most Asian cooking. Be careful when purchasing rice vermicelli as they can often be confused with cellophane noodles, sold in shiny white bundles. Look for the word rice or riz on the package.

SOBA NOODLES

Soba noodles

Brown or green in color, and found dried or fresh in Asian markets, soba noodles are made from buckwheat flour and water. Also known as buckwheat noodles, they are one of the most popular noodles eaten in Japan. Their nutty flavor also makes them delicious in summer salads and stir-fries. Soba noodles are more filling than other noodles, so a smaller quantity is usually prepared. If unavailable, use somen or rice vermicelli. Whole-wheat (wholemeal) spaghetti is also a good substitute.

Soups

Somen, pork and scallion soup

8 oz (250 g) somen noodles

4 cups (32 fl oz/1 L) chicken stock (page 100)

1 tablespoon dry sherry

1 tablespoon light soy sauce

6 scallions (shallots/spring onions), sliced

4 oz (125 g) Chinese barbecue pork, sliced

chili oil for serving

Cook noodles in boiling water until tender, about 3 minutes. Drain and divide among 4 individual bowls.

Place stock, sherry and soy sauce in saucepan. Bring to boil. Reduce heat to low and simmer for 5 minutes. Add scallions and pork. Cook for 1 minute.

Ladle soup over noodles. Pass chili oil at the table, to be added to taste.

Serves 4

SOMEN. PORK AND SCALLION SOUP

Coconut shrimp soup

1 lb (500 g) jumbo shrimp (king prawns)

1 lemongrass stalk, chopped, or 2 teaspoons grated lemon zest

1 carrot, peeled and sliced

1 celery stalk, sliced

1 onion, sliced

2 plum (Roma) tomatoes, chopped

1 bunch fresh cilantro (fresh coriander)

6 cups (48 fl oz/1.5 L) water

2 cups (16 fl oz/500 ml) coconut milk

1½ tablespoons red curry paste

1 teaspoon palm sugar or brown sugar

2 teaspoons fish sauce

8 oz (250 g) hokkien noodles

juice of 2 limes

Peel and devein shrimp; reserve heads and shells. Cover shrimp and set aside.

Place shrimp heads and shells in large saucepan. Add lemongrass or zest, carrot, celery, onion and tomatoes. Remove cilantro leaves from stems. Chop stems and add to saucepan; chop and reserve leaves. Pour in water. Bring to boil, reduce heat to low, cover and simmer gently, stirring occasionally, for 20 minutes. Strain through fine-mesh sieve. Measure 5 cups (40 fl oz/1.25 L) stock.

Return measured stock to saucepan. Stir in coconut milk, curry paste, sugar, fish sauce, noodles, lime juice, cilantro leaves and shrimp. Bring to boil, reduce heat to low, cover and simmer, stirring occasionally, until shrimp change color, 6–7 minutes.

Ladle into individual bowls and serve.

Serves 4

COCONUT SHRIMP SOUP

Chicken noodle soup

4 Chinese dried mushrooms

8 oz (250 g) egg noodles

¹/₂ cup (2 oz/60 g) shredded snow peas (mange-touts)

1 tablespoon vegetable oil

1 tablespoon light soy sauce

1 tablespoon rice wine

4 cups (32 fl oz/ 1 L) chicken stock (page 100)

1¹/₂ cups (8 oz/250 g) shredded cooked skinless chicken meat

¹/₂ cup (2 oz/60 g) fresh bean sprouts, rinsed

Place mushrooms in small bowl, add boiling water to cover and allow to stand until softened, 10–15 minutes. Drain and squeeze out excess liquid. Thinly slice mushrooms, discarding tough stems.

Cook egg noodles as directed on package or on page 12. Drain and set aside.

Place snow peas in bowl and add boiling water to cover. Let stand for 1 minute, then drain. Refresh snow peas immediately in cold water.

In wok or saucepan over medium-high heat, warm oil. Add sliced mushrooms and stir-fry for 1 minute. Add noodles, snow peas, soy sauce, rice wine, stock and chicken. Bring to boil over medium-high heat, stirring occasionally. Ladle into individual bowls. Garnish each serving with bean sprouts.

Serves 4

Combination short and long soup

3 1/2 oz (105 g) egg noodles

2 tablespoons vegetable oil

1 chicken breast fillet, skin removed

4 oz (125 g) ground (minced) chicken

1 cup (3 oz/90 g) shredded Chinese cabbage

1/4 cup (2 oz/60 g) chopped canned water chestnuts

2 teaspoons soy sauce

1 teaspoons Asian sesame oil

1 teaspoon peeled and grated fresh ginger

12 wonton wrappers

1 egg, beaten

6 cups (42 fl oz/ 1.5 L) chicken stock (page 100)

1 tablespoon dry sherry

12 jumbo shrimp (king prawns), peeled and
  deveined, tails intact

6 1/2 oz (200 g) baby spinach or bok choy, trimmed

4 oz (125 g) Chinese barbecue pork, sliced

soy sauce for serving

Notes

This traditional Chinese soup acquired its name from the use of noodles, which are long, and wonton dumplings, which are short, added to a clear broth. It is a meal on its own.

Cook noodles as directed on package or on page 12. Drain and set aside. Heat 1 tablespoon vegetable oil in wok or frying pan over medium heat. Add chicken breast and cook, turning once, until juices run clear when pierced with skewer, about 5 minutes on each side. Remove from pan and allow to cool. Slice chicken and set aside.

Heat remaining 1 tablespoon vegetable oil in same pan over medium-high heat. Add ground chicken and stir-fry until it changes color, about 5 minutes. Add cabbage and stir-fry for 2 minutes. Stir in water chestnuts, soy sauce, sesame oil and ginger. Remove from heat and let cool.

Place wonton wrappers on work surface and cover with damp kitchen towel. Working with one wrapper at a time, lay it on work surface and place 1 teaspoon ground chicken in middle. Brush edges with beaten egg, fold wrapper diagonally and curl around finger to form a tortellini-like shape. Set aside, covered with plastic wrap. Repeat with remaining wonton wrappers.

Combine chicken stock and sherry in saucepan. Bring to boil, reduce heat to low and simmer, uncovered, for 5 minutes. Add shrimp and wontons and simmer until shrimp change color, about 3 minutes. Stir in noodles, spinach or bok choy, pork and sliced chicken and simmer until noodles, pork and chicken are heated through, 4–5 minutes.

Ladle into individual bowls. Offer soy sauce at table, to be added to taste.

Serves 4

COMBINATION SHORT AND LONG SOUP

parcels

Mini noodle baskets with crab and avocado

4 oz (125 g) fresh thin egg noodles

vegetable oil for deep-frying

1 ripe avocado

juice of 1 lemon

4 oz (125 g) crabmeat, canned or fresh

4 oz (125 g) salmon roe

Hints

Noodle baskets not only look impressive but taste great. They can be made bite size or larger for serving individual portions. For this recipe, you can use a device specifically designed for making noodle nests and sold in Asian markets or specialty kitchen shops. Or you can use two heatproof strainers, one larger so that it holds the other. Be sure to dip the strainers in oil before putting the noodles in so they do not stick. The baskets can be made in advance of using and stored in an airtight container for up to five days.

Soak noodles in boiling water for 10 minutes. Drain and pat dry with paper towels.

Heat oil in wok or frying pan until it reaches 375°F (190°C) on deep-frying thermometer or until small bread cube dropped in oil sizzles and turns golden. Dip 2 strainers into oil to coat. Place 1 heaping tablespoon noodles in larger strainer. Press smaller strainer on top as firmly as possible. Plunge into oil and cook until golden and crisp, 1–2 minutes. Remove from oil. Lift basket from strainers and drain on paper towels. Repeat with remaining noodles. Set baskets aside and allow to cool. You should have 12 baskets.

Remove pit from avocado. Peel, cut into 12 thin slices and brush with lemon juice.

Place slice of avocado in each basket. Top with 1 teaspoon crabmeat and 1 teaspoon salmon roe. Serve immediately.

Makes 12 filled baskets

MINI NOODLE BASKETS WITH CRAB AND AVOCADO

Crispy fried wontons with chicken filling

FOR WONTONS

16 oz (500 g) ground (minced) chicken

2 teaspoons peeled and grated fresh ginger

4 scallions (shallots/spring onions), sliced

$^1/_4$ cup (2 oz/60 g) finely chopped canned water
   chestnuts

1 teaspoon Asian sesame oil

2 tablespoons soy sauce

1 tablespoon dry sherry

24 wonton wrappers

vegetable oil for deep-frying

FOR DIPPING SAUCE

1 tablespoon light soy sauce

1 teaspoon rice wine

1 teaspoon Asian sesame oil

1 tablespoon finely sliced scallions

(shallots/spring onions)

$^1/_2$ small red chili pepper, seeded and finely

chopped

$^1/_2$ teaspoon chili sauce

In bowl, combine chicken, ginger, scallions, water chestnuts, sesame oil, soy sauce and sherry. Mix well. Place wonton wrappers on work surface and cover with damp kitchen towel. Working with one wrapper at a time, lay it on work surface and place 1 teaspoon filling in middle. Brush edges with water. Gather wonton corners together and twist to seal. Set aside, covered with plastic wrap. Repeat with remaining wonton wrappers.

Heat vegetable oil in wok or frying pan until it reaches 375°F (190°C) on deep-frying thermometer or until small bread cube dropped in oil sizzles and turns golden. Working in batches if necessary, fry filled wontons until golden and crisp, 1–2 minutes. Using slotted spoon, remove from oil and drain on paper towels.

To make dipping sauce, combine soy sauce, rice wine, sesame oil, scallions, chili pepper and chili sauce. Mix well. Pour into serving dish and set aside.

Serve wontons hot with dipping sauce.

Serves 4

CRISPY FRIED WONTONS WITH CHICKEN FILLING

Deep fried shrimp balls

4 oz (125 g) rice vermicelli

2 lb (1 kg) jumbo shrimp (king prawns), peeled and deveined

1 tablespoon peeled and grated fresh ginger

1 teaspoon Asian sesame oil

1 egg, beaten

3 tablespoons cornstarch (cornflour)

¹/₄ cup (2 oz/60 g) finely chopped canned water chestnuts

2 tablespoons finely chopped scallions (shallots/spring onions)

3 tablespoons chopped fresh cilantro (fresh coriander)

vegetable oil for deep-frying

Thai sweet chili sauce for serving

lime wedges for serving

Place noodles in plastic bag and roughly break into 1-inch (2.5-cm) lengths. Set aside.

Place shrimp in a food processor or blender. Process until smooth. Add ginger, sesame oil, egg and cornstarch. Process to combine. Transfer shrimp mixture to bowl. Add water chestnuts, scallions and cilantro. Mix until well combined.

Using a teaspoon dipped in water, shape shrimp mixture into balls. You should have 16 balls. Roll balls in broken noodles, pressing gently to coat.

Heat vegetable oil in wok or frying pan until it reaches 375°F (190°C) on deep-frying thermometer or until small bread cube dropped in oil sizzles and turns golden. Working in batches if necessary, fry shrimp balls turning them so they cook evenly, until golden, 1–2 minutes. Using slotted spoon, remove from oil and drain on paper towels.

Serve shrimp balls hot with Thai sweet chili sauce and lime wedges.

Serves 4

Hint

Make sure you use rice stick noodles for this recipe. Cellophane (bean thread) noodles don't break up and do not fry as crisp.

DEEP FRIED SHRIMP BALLS

Pot stickers

8 oz (250 g) ground (minced) lean pork

1 onion, finely chopped

1 cup (3 oz/90 g) finely shredded green cabbage

2 teaspoons peeled and grated fresh ginger

1 tablespoon Asian sesame oil

1 tablespoon soy sauce

1 teaspoon white pepper

24 round wheat wonton wrappers

4 tablespoons vegetable oil

2 cups (16 fl oz/500 ml) chicken stock, or as needed

light soy sauce for serving

In a bowl, combine pork, onion, cabbage, ginger, sesame oil, soy sauce and pepper. Mix well.

Place wonton wrappers on work surface and cover with damp kitchen towel. Working with one wrapper at a time, lay it on work surface and place 1 teaspoon filling in middle. Brush edges with water, fold wonton in half and press edges together to seal. Using your fingertips, pinch frill around each folded wonton if desired. Set aside, covered with plastic wrap. Repeat with remaining wrappers.

Heat 1 tablespoon vegetable oil in heavy-bottomed pan over medium-high heat. Swirl to cover entire bottom of pan. Working in batches, fry filled wontons until golden brown on both sides, about 1 minute. Coat pan as needed with remaining 3 tablespoons vegetable oil.

Return pot stickers to pan and add enough stock to come halfway up sides of pot stickers. Cover and simmer until stock is almost absorbed, about 10 minutes. Uncover and cook until stock is completely absorbed and bottoms of pot stickers are crisp. Repeat with remaining pot stickers.

Serve pot stickers warm with soy sauce.

Serves 4

Notes

These panfried pork dumplings originally got their name because they tend to stick to the pot during cooking. Though messy, the dumplings have an authentic flavor and appearance.

Beef triangles

FOR TRIANGLES

2 oz (60 g) cellophane (bean thread) noodles

2 tablespoons olive oil

2 onions, finely diced

1 teaspoon ground cumin

1 teaspoon ground coriander

1 teaspoon ground turmeric

1 lb (500 g) lean ground (minced) beef

24 square egg wonton wrappers

1 egg, beaten

vegetable oil for deep-frying

FOR YOGURT DIPPING SAUCE

6 1/2 oz (200 g) plain (natural) yogurt

2 tablespoons chopped fresh mint

To make beef triangles, soak noodles in boiling water for 10 minutes. Drain well and set aside.

Heat olive oil in wok or frying pan over medium heat. Add onions and cook until slightly softened, about 1 minute. Add cumin, coriander and turmeric and cook, stirring, for 2 minutes. Stir in ground beef and cook, stirring, until meat changes color, 6–8 minutes. Remove from heat. Add drained noodles, mix well and allow to cool.

Place wonton wrappers on work surface and cover with damp kitchen towel. Working with one wrapper at a time, lay it on work surface and place 2 teaspoons filling in middle. Brush edges with beaten egg, fold diagonally and press edges together to seal. Set aside, covered with plastic wrap. Repeat with remaining wrappers.

Heat vegetable oil in wok or frying pan until it reaches 375°F (190°C) on deep-frying thermometer or until small bread cube dropped in oil sizzles and turns golden. Working in batches, fry wontons until golden and crisp, 1–2 minutes. Using slotted spoon, remove from oil and drain on absorbent paper. Repeat with remaining triangles.

To make dipping sauce, combine yogurt and mint in small bowl. Mix well. Spoon into serving dish and chill in refrigerator for 30 minutes.

Serve triangles hot with dipping sauce.

Serves 4

Notes

These delicoius, bite-size snacks are seasoned with Indian spices. They are a great way to use leftover ground beef.

BEEF TRIANGLES

NOODLE CRAB CAKES

Thai beef salad

FOR SALAD

1 lb (500 g) sirloin (rump) steak

2 tablespoons soy sauce

2 cloves garlic, crushed

1 tablespoon rice wine

2 tablespoons olive oil

4 oz (125 g) thin egg noodles

4 oz (125 g) green beans, trimmed and blanched

½ English (hothouse) cucumber, seeded and thinly sliced

3 small red chili peppers, seeded and sliced

2 tablespoons chopped fresh cilantro (fresh coriander)

2 tablespoons fresh mint leaves

1 cup (4 oz/125 g) fresh bean spouts or mung beans, rinsed

1 cup (4 oz/125 g) unsalted roasted peanuts

FOR DRESSING

2 tablespoons lime juice

2 tablespoons fish sauce

1 clove garlic, crushed

1 tablespoon palm sugar or brown sugar

Place steak in glass or ceramic bowl. Combine soy sauce, garlic and rice wine, pour over steak and turn to coat with marinade. Cover and marinate for 30 minutes. Drain steak and pat dry with paper towels.

In a frying pan over high heat, warm oil. When hot, add steak and cook until light brown on outside and rare on inside, about 2 minutes on each side. Allow steak to cool, then thinly slice across grain and set aside.

Cook noodles as directed on package or on page 12. Drain and allow to cool.

In bowl, combine steak, noodles, green beans, cucumber, chili peppers, cilantro, mint, bean sprouts or mung beans and peanuts.

To make dressing, place lime juice, fish sauce, garlic and palm or brown sugar into jar with screw top. Shake well and set aside.

Add dressing to salad, toss gently and serve.

Serves 4

Tuna and red onion salad

FOR DRESSING

1 small red chili pepper, seeded, if desired, and
  thinly sliced, or 1 teaspoon chili sauce

1 clove garlic, crushed

grated zest of 1 lime

1 tablespoon lime juice

2 tablespoons olive oil

1 tablespoon balsamic vinegar

FOR SALAD

6$\frac{1}{2}$ oz (200 g) rice stick, somen, udon or soba
  noodles

6 oz (185 g) canned tuna in oil, drained and flaked

1 red onion, chopped

$\frac{1}{4}$ cup ($\frac{1}{3}$ oz/10 g) chopped fresh cilantro (fresh
  coriander)

To make dressing, place chili, garlic, lime zest and juice, olive oil and vinegar in jar with screw top. Shake well and set aside.

To make salad, cook noodles as directed on package or on page 12. Drain and allow to cool.

In bowl, combine noodles, tuna, onion and cilantro. Mix well.

Add dressing and toss until well combined. Cover and refrigerate for 30 minutes to blend flavors.

Spoon into individual bowls and serve chilled.

Serves 4

Hints

We used thick spaghetti in this recipe, you can also use rice stick, somen , udon or soba noodles.

Chicken and udon noodle salad

FOR DRESSING

2 tablespoons lime juice

2 teaspoons fish sauce (optional)

1 tablespoon mirin

2 teaspoons brown sugar or palm sugar

1 tablespoon peanut oil

FOR SALAD

1 cup (8 fl oz/250 ml) coconut milk

1/2 cup (4 fl oz/125 ml) water

2 small red chili peppers, halved and seeded

1 lemongrass stalk, roughly chopped, or 1
   teaspoon grated lemon zest

2 skinless chicken breast fillets

5 oz (150 g) udon noodles or spaghetti

1/2 red bell pepper (capsicum), seeded and
   chopped

1 carrot, peeled and grated

3 oz (90 g) snow peas (mange-tout), blanched
   and sliced

1 English (hothouse) cucumber, halved, seeded
   and sliced

3 tablespoons chopped fresh cilantro (fresh
   coriander), plus leaves for garnish

To make dressing, combine lime juice, fish sauce (if using), mirin, sugar and oil in jar with screw top. Shake well and set aside.

Place coconut milk, water, chili peppers, lemongrass or zest and chicken in saucepan. Bring to boil, reduce heat to low and simmer until chicken is tender, 7–8 minutes. Remove from heat and allow chicken to cool in liquid.

Drain and discard cooking liquid. Thinly slice chicken.

Cook noodles as directed on package or on page 12. Drain and allow to cool.

In bowl, combine chicken, noodles, bell pepper, carrot, snow peas, cucumber and chopped cilantro. Mix well. Add dressing and toss until well combined. Cover and refrigerate for 30 minutes to blend flavors.

Spoon onto individual plates and garnish each serving with cilantro leaves.

Serves 4

Hints

You can use spaghetti in place of udon noodles. Substitute lemon grass with grated rind of 1 lemon if unavailable.

CHICKEN AND UDON NOODLE SALAD

Crispy noodle salad

2 oz (60 g) cellophane (bean thread) noodles or rice vermicelli

vegetable oil for deep-frying

1 tablespoon sesame seeds

2 tablespoons sunflower seeds

2 tablespoons pumpkin seeds

4 cups (12 oz/375 g) shredded red cabbage

1 red bell pepper (capsicum), seeded and sliced

1 green bell pepper (capsicum), seeded and sliced

3 oz (90 g) button mushrooms (champignons), brushed clean and halved

4 scallions (shallots/spring onions), sliced

Preheat oven to 400°F (200°C/Gas 6). Break or cut noodles into small bundles. Heat oil in wok or frying pan until it reaches 375°F (190°C) on deep-frying thermometer or until small bread cube dropped in oil sizzles and turns golden. Working in batches, fry noodles until golden, 30 seconds. Using slotted spoon, remove from oil and drain on paper towels.

Place sesame seeds, sunflower seeds and pumpkin seeds on baking sheet and toast until golden, 4–5 minutes. Allow to cool.

In large bowl, combine cabbage, bell peppers, mushrooms, scallions, toasted seeds and noodles. Gently toss until well combined. Serve immediately. (Noodles will loose crisp texture if left to stand for too long.)

Serves 4

CRISPY NOODLE SALAD

Baked chicken wings with noodle stuffing

$3^1/_2$ oz (105 g) cellophane (bean thread) noodles

8 oz (250 g) ground (minced) chicken

1 teaspoon peeled and grated fresh ginger

1 clove garlic, finely chopped

2 teaspoons rice wine or dry sherry

1 tablespoon finely chopped fresh cilantro (fresh coriander)

12 large chicken wings

2 tablespoons soy sauce

1 tablespoon honey

cucumber slices for serving

Thai sweet chili sauce for serving

Soak noodles in boiling water for 10 minutes; drain. In bowl, combine noodles, ground chicken, ginger, garlic, rice wine or sherry and cilantro. Mix well.

Preheat oven to 350°F (180°C/Gas 4). Oil baking dish large enough to accommodate wings in one layer.

Using small sharp knife, remove small drumstick from each chicken wing (and reserve for another use), leaving wing tip and middle section intact. Starting at top of middle joint (opposite end to wing tip), start gently separating skin from bone until you reach joint. Remove and discard bone. You should now have wing tip with cavity of skin attached. Fill each cavity with about 1 tablespoon chicken stuffing and close. Place into prepared baking dish. Repeat with remaining wings.

In small bowl, combine soy sauce and honey. Brush on wings. Bake until golden and tender, about 20 minutes.

Serve hot or cold, garnished with cucumber slices. Pass chili sauce at table.

Serves 4

BAKED CHICKEN WINGS WITH NOODLE STUFFING

Chicken and noodles in crisp lettuce cups

2 Chinese dried mushrooms

3^1/$_2$ oz (105 g) cellophane (bean thread) noodles

1 tablespoon vegetable oil

2 small red chili peppers, seeded, if desired, and chopped

2 cloves garlic, crushed

12 oz (375 g) ground (minced) chicken

6 scallions (shallots/spring onions), sliced

^{1}/$_4$ cup (1 oz/30 g) finely chopped canned bamboo shoots

^{1}/$_4$ cup (2 oz/60 g) finely chopped canned water chestnuts

juice of 1 lime

2 tablespoons fish sauce

2 tablespoons chopped fresh mint

3 tablespoons chopped fresh cilantro (fresh coriander)

1 tablespoon Asian sesame oil

1 small head butter or iceberg lettuce, leaves separated and trimmed

Thai sweet chili sauce for serving

Place mushrooms in small bowl, add boiling water to cover and let stand for 10–15 minutes. Drain and squeeze out excess liquid. Finely chop mushrooms, discarding tough stems.

Soak noodles in boiling water for 10 minutes. Drain and set aside.

In frying pan over medium-high heat, warm vegetable oil. Add chili pepper and garlic and cook until aromatic, about 1 minute. Add ground chicken and mushrooms and cook, stirring occasionally, until chicken is browned, 4–5 minutes. Remove from heat and stir in noodles, scallions, bamboo shoots, water chestnuts, lime juice, fish sauce, mint, cilantro and sesame oil. Mix well.

To serve, arrange lettuce leaves on individual plates. Spoon chicken mixture on leaves. Drizzle with chili sauce.

Serves 4

Thai basil chicken

5 oz (150 g) cellophane (bean thread) noodles or
    rice vermicelli

2 tablespoons fish sauce

1 tablespoon rice wine

5 cloves garlic, crushed

2 tablespoons finely chopped scallions
    (shallots/green onions)

1 lb (500 g) skinless chicken breast fillets, sliced

2 tablespoons vegetable oil

1 small red chili pepper, seeded, if desired, and
    chopped.

1 red bell pepper (capsicum), seeded and sliced

1 red onion, sliced

2 tablespoons soy sauce

1 tablespoon water

2 teaspoons palm sugar or brown sugar

¹/₂ cup (1/2 oz/15 g) fresh basil leaves

Soak noodles in boiling water for 10 minutes; drain. In bowl, combine fish sauce, rice wine, 2 cloves garlic and scallions. Add chicken and stir to coat with marinade. Cover and allow to marinate in refrigerator for 1 hour. Drain.

In wok or frying pan over medium-high heat, warm oil. Add remaining 3 cloves garlic and chili pepper. Cook until aromatic, about 1 minute. Add chicken and cook until tender, 4–5 minutes. Reduce heat to medium and stir in bell pepper, onion, noodles, soy sauce, water and sugar. Cook, stirring occasionally, until noodles are heated through, about 2 minutes. Remove from heat and stir in basil.

Spoon into individual bowls and serve immediately.

Serves 4

THAI BASIL CHICKEN

Roasted duck with noodle stuffing

6¹/₂ oz (200 g) somen noodles

1 duck, about 4 lb (2 kg)

1 tablespoon olive oil

1 onion, finely chopped

10 oz (300 g) ground (minced) chicken

8 fresh shiitake mushrooms, brushed clean and
 sliced

2 tablespoons soy sauce

2 tablespoons oyster sauce

2 teaspoons palm sugar or brown sugar

1 tablespoon dry sherry

¹/₄ cup (2 oz/60 g) finely chopped canned water
 chestnuts

Cook noodles as directed on package or on page 12. Drain and allow to cool.

Preheat oven to 400°F (200°C/Gas 6). Lightly oil roasting pan and place rack in pan.

Rinse duck and pat dry with paper towels. Trim off excess fat.

In wok or frying pan over medium-high heat, warm oil. Add onion and cook until softened, about 2 minutes. Add ground chicken, cook, stirring, until meat changes color, about 5 minutes. Stir in mushrooms, soy and oyster sauces, sugar, sherry and water chestnuts. Cook for 1 minute. Remove from heat and allow to cool. Stir in noodles.

Spoon stuffing into duck cavity. Secure and truss with kitchen string. Place on rack in prepared pan. Using fork, prick duck skin all over. Bake for 15 minutes. Reduce heat to 350°F (180°C/Gas 4) and cook until juices run clear when skewer is inserted in thigh, about 1 hour. Remove from oven and let stand for about 10 minutes.

Remove stuffing from duck and place in serving bowl. Carve duck and serve with stuffing.

Serves 4–6

Hints

You can substitute with a large chicken if desired.

Accompany with steamed bok choy or other Chinese greens.

ROASTED DUCK WITH NOODLE STUFFING

Sweet-and-sour chicken and noodles

8 oz (250 g) rice stick noodles

vegetable oil for deep-frying, plus 2 tablespoons

8 oz (250 g) skinless chicken breast fillet, cut into
1-inch (2.5-cm) pieces

1 onion, sliced

2 tablespoons tomato paste (purée)

2 tablespoons palm sugar or brown sugar

1 tablespoon fish sauce

3 tablespoons lime juice

1 piece grapefruit zest, 2 inches (5 cm) long,
shredded

2 tablespoons water

2 tablespoons fresh cilantro (fresh coriander) leaves

thin strips grapefruit zest for garnish

lime wedges for serving

Place noodles in plastic bag and roughly break up into bite-sized pieces.

Heat oil in wok or frying pan until it reaches 375°F (190°C) on deep-frying thermometer or until small bread cube dropped in oil sizzles and turns golden. Working in batches if necessary, add noodles and fry until golden and crisp, about 30 seconds. Using slotted spoon, remove from pan and drain on paper towels.

In another frying pan over medium-high heat, warm 2 tablespoons oil. Add chicken and cook, stirring occasionally, until golden, 4–5 minutes. Remove from pan. Add onion to same pan and cook until softened, about 2 minutes.

In small bowl, combine tomato paste, sugar, fish sauce, lime juice, shredded zest and water. Add to pan, reduce heat to low and simmer, stirring occasionally, until sauce thickens, 3–4 minutes. Stir in chicken and noodles, raise heat to medium and cook until heated through, 1–2 minutes.

To serve, spoon chicken and noodles onto individual plates. Sprinkle with cilantro leaves and garnish with zest strips. Accompany with lime wedges.

Serves 4

SWEET-AND-SOUR CHICKEN AND NOODLES 55

CHICKEN SATAY SALAD 57

SHRIMP AND GLASS NOODLE STEW

Salmon with sweet pepper sauce

3 tablespoons vegetable oil

1 small red chili pepper, seeded and chopped

2 cloves garlic, crushed

1 red bell pepper (capsicum), seeded and diced

2 tablespoons palm sugar or brown sugar

1 tablespoon rice vinegar

1 tablespoon soy sauce

1 cup (8 fl oz/250 ml) water

2 teaspoons cornstarch (cornflour) combined with
   1 tablespoon water

2 teaspoons lemon juice

$6^1/_2$ oz (180 g) egg noodles

3 teaspoons Asian sesame oil

1 tablespoon lime juice

2 tablespoons chopped fresh cilantro (fresh
   coriander)

4 salmon fillets, $6^1/_2$ oz (200 g) each

In wok or frying pan over medium-high heat, warm 1 tablespoon of vegetable oil. Add chili pepper, garlic and bell pepper and cook, stirring occasionally, until bell pepper is softened, about 3 minutes. Stir in sugar, vinegar, soy sauce and water. Reduce heat to low and simmer until flavors are blended, about 5 minutes. Stir in cornstarch and water. Continuing to stir, bring sauce to boil and cook until thickened, 2–3 minutes. Remove from heat and stir in lemon juice.

Cook noodles as directed on package or on page 12. Drain. In small bowl, combine sesame oil, lime juice and cilantro. Mix well. Pour over noodles and toss to coat.

In frying pan over medium-high heat, warm remaining 2 tablespoons vegetable oil. Add salmon fillets and cook until fish flakes easily when tested with fork, 2–3 minutes on each side.

To serve, reheat sweet pepper sauce if necessary. Arrange noodles and salmon fillets on individual plates. Spoon sauce on top and serve immediately.

Serves 4

SALMON WITH SWEET PEPPER SAUCE

Seafood hot pot

8 cups (64 fl oz/2 L) fish stock (page 101)

1 piece fresh ginger, 2 inches (5 cm) long, peeled

1 teaspoon chili paste

2 tablespoons Asian sesame oil

2 lb (1 kg) jumbo shrimp (king prawns), peeled
   and deveined, tails intact

8 oz (250 g) firm white-fleshed fish fillets, cut
   into bite-size pieces

8 oz (250 g) squid rings

6¹/₂ oz (200 g) scallops, cleaned

2 small bok choy, leaves separated and trimmed

4 oz (125 g) snow peas (mange-touts), trimmed

6¹/₂ oz (200 g) egg noodles

Place stock in saucepan. Bring to boil, reduce heat to low and simmer for 5 minutes. Add ginger, chili paste and sesame oil and simmer until flavors are blended, about 5 minutes. Transfer stock to hot pot. Arrange the seafood and vegetables on a platter, and place platter and hot pot on table.

Using chopsticks, guests dip seafood and vegetables into hot stock and cook until tender, 1–2 minutes.

After seafood and vegetables are cooked, add noodles to stock and cook until tender, about 3 minutes. Stock and noodles are then ladled into individual bowls and served.

Serves 4

Hints

For this recipe, you will need a hot pot, which keeps the aromatic stock hot at the table. In place of chopsticks, small wire baskets with handles can be used to cook the seafood and vegetables in the simmering stock. Look for these items in Asian specialty stores. A fondue set or an electric frying pan can also be used if a traditional hot pot is unavailable.

Seafood laksa

6½ oz (200 g) cellophane (bean thread) noodles

1 onion, roughly chopped

3 cloves garlic

1 piece fresh ginger, 2 inches (5 cm) long, peeled

2 teaspoons ground turmeric

2 tablespoons vegetable oil

1 teaspoon grated lemon zest

1¾ cups (14 fl oz/440 ml) coconut milk

3 cups (24 fl oz/750 ml) fish stock (page 101)

1 lb (500 g) jumbo shrimp (king prawns), peeled and deveined, tails intact

8 oz (250 g) firm white-fleshed fish fillets, cut into 1-inch (2.5-cm) cubes

10 mussels in shell, scrubbed and debearded

4 small red chili peppers, halved and seeded

1 cup (4 oz/125 g) fresh bean sprouts, rinsed

2 tablespoons chopped fresh cilantro (fresh coriander)

6 scallions (shallots/green onions), julienned

Soak noodles in boiling water for 10 minutes. Drain and set aside. Place onion, garlic, ginger and turmeric in food processor or blender. Process until smooth. In wok or saucepan over medium-high heat, warm oil. Add onion paste and cook for approximately 3 minutes. Add lemon zest, coconut milk and stock. Bring to boil, reduce heat to low and simmer until flavors are blended, about 5 minutes.

Stir in shrimp, fish cubes, mussels and chili peppers. Simmer until shrimp change color, about 5 minutes. Discard any mussels that do not open.

To serve, divide noodles, bean sprouts, cilantro and scallions among individual bowls. Top with seafood and broth. Serve immediately.

Serves 4

Hint

For a traditional laksa, add extra chopped red chili pepper, fresh mint and fresh cilantro just before serving.

Pad thai

5 oz (150 g) thick rice stick noodles

5 tablespoons vegetable oil

4 oz (125 g) firm tofu, cut into 1-inch (2.5-cm) cubes

2 cloves garlic, crushed

1 lb (500 g) jumbo shrimp (king prawns), peeled and deveined, tails intact

3 tablespoons lemon juice

2 tablespoons fish sauce

3 tablespoons palm sugar or brown sugar

2 eggs, beaten

2 tablespoons chopped chives

2 tablespoons chopped fresh cilantro (fresh coriander)

2 tablespoons chopped fresh basil

2 tablespoons fried onion

lemon wedges for serving

Cook noodles as directed on package or on page 12. Drain and set aside. In wok or frying pan over medium-high heat, warm oil. Add tofu and cook, stirring constantly, until golden, 1–2 minutes. Drain on paper towels. Drain all but 2 tablespoons oil from pan and return to medium-high heat. Add garlic and shrimp and cook, stirring occasionally, until shrimp change color, 4–5 minutes. Add lemon juice, fish sauce and sugar, stirring until sugar dissolves. Mix in noodles.

Push noodle mixture to one side of wok or pan. Add eggs and cook, without stirring, until partially set. Then stir gently until scrambled. Stir egg through noodle mixture. Add tofu, chives, cilantro and basil. Cook until heated through, about 1 minute.

To serve, divide among individual plates and sprinkle with fried onion. Accompany with lemon wedges.

Serves 4

Chili squid salad

FOR SALAD

8 oz (250 g) rice stick noodles

4 squid bodies, about 12 oz (375 g)

2 cups (16 fl oz/500 ml) fish stock (page 101)

$^1/_2$ cup (4 fl oz/125 ml) dry white wine

1 onion, cut into eighths

4 tomatoes, chopped

$^1/_4$ cup (1/3 oz/10 g) chopped fresh cilantro (fresh
coriander)

$^1/_4$ cup (3/4 oz/20 g) chopped fresh mint

$^1/_4$ cup (1 oz/30 g) chopped scallions
(shallots/green onions)

FOR DRESSING

1–2 small red chili peppers, seeded, if desired,
and halved

3 cloves garlic

1 teaspoon Tabasco sauce

$^1/_4$ cup (2 fl oz/60 ml) fish sauce

5 tablespoons lime juice

To make salad, cook noodles as directed on package or on page 9. Drain and allow to cool.

Cut squid half lengthwise. Cut shallow slashes in crisscross pattern on inside of squid. Then cut into strips ¾ inch (2 cm) wide. Place stock and wine in saucepan. Bring to boil, reduce heat to low, add squid and cook until tender, 1–2 minutes. Do not overcook or squid will become tough. Drain and allow to cool.

In large bowl, combine noodles, squid, onion, tomatoes, cilantro, mint and scallions. Add dressing, toss, cover and refrigerate for 1 hour before serving.

To make dressing, combine chili peppers to taste, garlic, Tabasco, fish sauce and lime juice in food processor or blender. Process until smooth. Set aside.

To serve, divide chilled salad among individual plates.

Serves 4

CHILI SQUID SALAD   6 9

CHINESE BARBECUE PORK STIR-FRY   7 1

Stir-fried beef with eggs

8 oz (250 g) egg noodles

4 tablespoons vegetable oil

3 cloves garlic, crushed

1/4 cup (1 oz/30 g) chopped scallions
(shallots/green onions)

8 oz (250 g) lean ground (minced) beef

3 tablespoons water

1 tablespoon soy sauce

1 tablespoon oyster sauce

1 teaspoon cornstarch (cornflour) mixed with
1 tablespoon water

4 butter lettuce leaves, trimmed

4 eggs, soft-boiled, peeled and halved

1/4 cup (1/3 oz/10 g) fresh mint leaves

Cook noodles as directed on package or on page 12. Drain and pat dry with paper towels.

In wok or frying pan over medium-high heat, warm 3 tablespoons of oil. Add garlic and cook until aromatic, about 1 minute. Add noodles and stir-fry for 2 minutes. Remove from wok or pan. Add remaining 1 tablespoon oil to wok or pan over medium-high heat. Add scallions and ground beef and stir-fry until meat changes color, 3–4 minutes. Add water, soy and oyster sauces and noodles and stir-fry for 3 minutes. Stir in cornstarch and water and cook, stirring, until sauce thickens, about 2 minutes.

To serve, arrange lettuce leaves on individual plates. Spoon beef and noodles on top. Garnish with egg halves and mint leaves. Serve immediately.

Serves 4

Beef chow mein

6½ oz (200 g) wheat flour, rice stick or thick egg
   noodles

2 tablespoons soy sauce

3 tablespoons hoisin sauce

2 cloves garlic, crushed

2 teaspoons peeled and grated fresh ginger

12 oz (375 g) round (topside) or sirloin (rump)
   steak, thinly sliced

2 tablespoons vegetable oil

8 fresh shiitake mushrooms, brushed clean and
   sliced

6 scallions (shallots/green onions), sliced

6 oz (180 g) broccoli, cut into florets

2 tablespoons beef stock

1 tablespoon dry sherry

1 teaspoon Asian sesame oil

Cook noodles as directed on package or on pages 6–11. Drain and set aside. In glass or ceramic bowl, combine soy and hoisin sauces, garlic and ginger. Add steak slices, turn to coat in marinade, cover and marinate for 30 minutes. Drain and reserve marinade.

In wok or frying pan over medium-high heat, warm vegetable oil. Add steak and stir-fry until meat changes color, 3–4 minutes. Remove from pan. Return pan to medium-high heat, add mushrooms, scallions and broccoli, and stir-fry for 2 minutes. Add noodles, steak, reserved marinade, stock, sherry and sesame oil. Cook until heated through, 1–2 minutes.

Serve immediately, divided among individual plates.

Serves 4–6

BEEF CHOW MEIN

Steamed pork buns

4 Chinese dried mushrooms

1 lb (500 g) lean ground (minced) pork

10 canned water chestnuts, finely chopped

1 tablespoon peeled and grated fresh ginger

1½ tablespoons rice wine

2 teaspoons soy sauce

2 teaspoons Asian sesame oil

2 cloves garlic, crushed

1 teaspoon superfine (caster) sugar

24 wonton wrappers

oyster sauce for serving

Place mushrooms in small bowl, add boiling water to cover and allow to stand for 10–15 minutes. Drain and squeeze out excess liquid. Finely chop mushrooms, discarding tough stems.

In bowl, combine pork, mushrooms, water chestnuts, ginger, rice wine, soy sauce, sesame oil, garlic and sugar. Using moistened hands, mix until well combined.

Place wonton wrappers on work surface and cover with damp kitchen towel. Working with one wrapper at a time, lay it on work surface and place 1 teaspoon pork filling in middle. Brush edges with water, gather edges together and squeeze to form a bundle. Set aside, covered with plastic wrap. Repeat with remaining wonton wrappers.

Place filled wontons on lightly greased steamer rack in saucepan or wok of boiling water. Cover and steam for 20 minutes. (You may need to do this in batches).

Serve hot with oyster sauce.

Serves 4

STEAMED PORK BUNS

Korean beef rolls

vegetable oil for deep-frying, plus 1 tablespoon

3½ oz (105 g) cellophane (bean thread) noodles
   or rice vermicelli

4 cloves garlic, crushed

1 tablespoon peeled and grated fresh ginger

1 small red chili pepper, seeded, if desired, and
   chopped, or 1 teaspoon chili paste

12 oz (375 g) lean ground (minced) beef

¼ cup (1 oz/30 g) chopped scallions
   (shallots/green onions)

2 teaspoons Asian sesame oil

5 oz (150 g) firm tofu, finely chopped

12 butter lettuce leaves, trimmed

12 scallions (shallots/green onions), blanched
   (optional)

Thai sweet chili sauce for serving

Heat vegetable oil in wok or frying pan until it reaches 375°F (190°C) on deep-frying thermometer or until small bread cube dropped in oil sizzles and turns golden. Working in small batches, add noodles and fry until crisp, about 30 seconds. Using slotted spoon, remove from pan and drain on paper towels.

In wok or frying pan over medium-high heat, warm 1 tablespoon vegetable oil. Add garlic, ginger and chili pepper and stir-fry until aromatic, approximately 1 minute. Add ground beef and cook, stirring, until meat changes color, 3–4 minutes. Stir in chopped scallions, sesame oil and tofu and cook 1 minute.

Place lettuce leaf on work surface. Spoon small amount of crisp noodles and beef mixture on leaf. Roll up; tie with blanched scallion if desired. Repeat with remaining lettuce leaves.

Divide rolls among individual plates, placing them seam side down, and accompany with Thai sweet chili sauce. The ingredients can be served in separate bowls, and guests can assemble their own rolls.

Serves 4

KOREAN BEEF ROLLS

Beef stir fry on crisp noodles

vegetable oil for deep-frying, plus 1 tablespoon

8 oz (250 g) fresh thin egg noodles

1 tablespoon soy sauce

3 cloves garlic, chopped

12 oz (375 g) sirloin (rump) steak, thinly sliced

2 onions, cut into eighths

6–7 oz (180–220 g) asparagus, trimmed and cut
    into 1-inch (2.5-cm) pieces

2 tablespoons oyster sauce

1 teaspoon cornstarch (cornflour) mixed with
    2 tablespoons beef stock

Heat oil in wok or frying pan until it reaches 375°F (190°C) on deep-frying thermometer or until small bread cube dropped in oil sizzles and turns golden. Working in batches, add noodles and fry until crisp, about 30 seconds. Using a slotted spoon, remove from pan and drain on paper towels.

In glass or ceramic bowl, combine soy sauce and garlic. Add steak slices, turn to coat with marinade, cover and marinate for 30 minutes. Drain and reserve marinade.

In wok or frying pan over medium-high heat, warm 1 tablespoon oil. Add steak and stir-fry until meat changes color, 3–4 minutes, remove from pan. Return pan to medium-high heat, add onion and stir-fry until softened, about 2 minutes. Return meat to pan, add asparagus and cook until asparagus is tender-crisp, about 2 minutes. Stir in oyster sauce and cornstarch and stock. Continuing to stir, cook until sauce thickens, 1–2 minutes.

To serve, arrange noodles on individual plates. Top with beef stir-fry and serve immediately.

Serves 4

Hint

Freeze the steak in a plastic bag for 20 minutes to make it easier to slice thinly. Cut across the grain to promote tenderness.

Pork curry on noodles

8 oz (250 g) lean ground (minced) pork

4 cloves garlic, crushed

2 lemongrass stalks, chopped, or grated zest of 1
   lemon

1 tablespoon peeled and grated fresh ginger

1 tablespoon vegetable oil

1 tablespoon green curry paste or to taste

1¹/₂ cups (12 fl oz/375 ml) coconut milk

1 cup (8 fl oz/250 ml) chicken stock (page 100)

2 tablespoons fish sauce

2 teaspoons palm sugar or brown sugar

8 oz (250 g) hokkien noodles

¹/₂ cup (³/₄ oz/20 g) fresh basil leaves, plus basil
   leaves for serving

4 scallions (shallots/green onions), chopped

¹/₄ cup (¹/₃ oz/10g) chopped fresh cilantro (fresh
   coriander)

In bowl, combine ground pork, garlic, lemongrass or zest and ginger. Using moistened hands, mix until well combined. Shape into walnut-size balls.

In wok or frying pan over medium-high heat, warm oil. Add curry paste and cook until aromatic, about 1 minute. Stir in coconut milk and stock. Reduce heat to low and simmer gently for 3 minutes. Raise heat to medium and add pork balls, fish sauce and sugar. Cook, stirring occasionally, until pork changes color, about 5 minutes.

Cook noodles as directed on package or on page 8. Drain.

Arrange noodles in individual soup or pasta bowls. Stir ½ cup (¾ oz/20 g) basil leaves, scallions and cilantro into curry. Spoon over noodles and garnish with fresh basil leaves. Serve immediately.

Serves 4

PORK CURRY ON NOODLES

Noodles with squash and green papaya

250 g (8 oz) rice stick noodles

2 tablespoons vegetable oil

2 cloves garlic, crushed

1 lb (500 g) butternut squash (pumpkin), peeled
and cut into 1-inch (2.5-cm) cubes

13 oz (400 g) green papaya, grated

$^3/_4$ cup (6 fl oz/180 ml) chicken stock (page 100)

2 eggs, beaten

2 tablespoons fish sauce

Cook noodles as directed on package or on page 12. Drain and set aside. In wok or frying pan over medium-high heat, warm oil. Add garlic and squash and cook until garlic is golden, about 2 minutes. Add papaya and stock. Reduce heat to low and simmer, covered, until pumpkin is tender and stock is absorbed, about 15 minutes.

Push pumpkin mixture to one side of wok or pan and raise heat to medium. Add eggs and cook, without stirring, until partially set. Stir gently until eggs are scrambled. Stir eggs into pumpkin mixture. Stir in noodles and fish sauce. Cook until heated through, about 1 minute.

Divide among individual plates and serve immediately.

Serves 4

Hints

Wear rubber gloves and lightly oil your grater when grating the green papaya, as it gets quite sticky.

NOODLES WITH SQUASH AND GREEN PAPAYA

Fried tofu salad

FOR SALAD

8 oz (250 g) egg noodles

1 English (hothouse) cucumber, thinly sliced

1 red bell pepper (capsicum), seeded and sliced

1 cup (4 oz/125 g) fresh bean sprouts, rinsed

3 tablespoons sliced scallions (shallots/green onions)

2 tablespoons sesame seeds, toasted

3 tablespoons vegetable oil

6 1/2 oz (200 g) firm tofu, cut into 1-inch (2.5-cm) cubes

FOR DRESSING

2 cloves garlic

1 piece fresh ginger, 1-inch (2.5-cm) long, peeled

6 tablespoons crunchy peanut butter

1 tablespoon Asian sesame oil

3 tablespoon rice wine

1 tablespoon Worcestershire sauce

3 teaspoons palm sugar or brown sugar

5 tablespoons chicken stock (page 100)

Cook noodles as directed on package or on page 12. Drain and allow to cool.

In large bowl, combine cucumber, bell pepper, bean sprouts, scallions and sesame seeds. Cover and chill.

In wok or frying pan over medium-high heat, warm oil. Add tofu and cook, stirring constantly, until golden, 3–4 minutes. Drain on paper towels and allow to cool.

Add tofu and noodles to bowl. Add dressing and toss until well combined.

To make dressing, place garlic, ginger, peanut butter, sesame oil, rice wine, Worcestershire sauce, sugar and stock in food processor. Process 10 seconds.

Cover salad and refrigerate for 30 minutes.

To serve, divide chilled salad among individual plates.

Serves 4

FRIED TOFU SALAD

VEGETARIAN SPRING ROLLS

Soba noodles with bell peppers

6 1/2 oz (200 g) soba noodles

1 tablespoon vegetable oil

2 teaspoons Asian sesame oil

3 cloves garlic, crushed

2 teaspoons peeled and grated fresh ginger

1/2 teaspoon red pepper flakes

1 onion, chopped

1 red bell pepper (capsicum), seeded and sliced

1 yellow bell pepper (capsicum), seeded and sliced

2 small zucchini (courgettes), julienned

5 oz (150 g) green beans, trimmed

3 tablespoons soy sauce

2 tablespoons rice wine

3 teaspoons palm sugar or brown sugar

1 1/2 tablespoons Worcestershire sauce

1/3 cup (1 1/2 oz/45 g) unsalted roasted peanuts, chopped

In wok or frying pan over medium-high heat, warm vegetable and sesame oils. Add garlic, ginger, red pepper flakes and onion and cook until aromatic, about 1 minute. Add bell peppers, zucchini and beans and stir-fry until slightly softened, about 3 minutes. Combine soy sauce, rice wine, sugar, Worcestershire sauce and noodles. Add to wok or pan and stir-fry until heated through, about 2 minutes.

To serve, divide among individual plates and top with peanuts. Serve immediately.

Serves 4

SOBA NOODLES WITH BELL PEPPERS

Sweet date wontons

6¹/₂ oz (200 g) dates, pitted and chopped

¹/₂ cup (2 oz/60 g) walnuts, chopped

6¹/₂ oz (200 g) fresh or canned lychees, pitted and
  chopped

1 tablespoon grated orange zest

24 wonton wrappers

1 egg, beaten

vegetable oil for deep-frying

2 tablespoons confectioners' (icing) sugar, sifted

In bowl, combine dates, walnuts, lychees and orange zest. Mix well. Place wonton wrappers on work surface and cover with damp kitchen towel. Working with one wrapper at a time, lay on work surface and place 1 teaspoon filling in middle. Brush edges of wonton with egg, gather edges and twist to seal. Repeat with remaining wonton wrappers.

Heat oil in wok or frying pan until it reaches 375°F (190°C) on deep-frying thermometer or until small bread cube dropped in oil sizzles and turns golden. Working in batches if necessary, add wontons and fry until golden, 1–2 minutes. Using slotted spoon, remove from pan and drain on paper towels. Allow to cool.

Sprinkled with confectioners' sugar and serve.

Makes 24 wontons

SWEET DATE WONTONS

Cream and berry stack

vegetable oil for deep-frying

8 wonton wrappers

8 oz (250 g) ricotta cheese

$^1/_2$ cup (4 fl oz/125 ml) heavy (double) cream

4 tablespoons confectioners' (icing) sugar, sifted

2 teaspoons Grand Marnier

1 teaspoon grated orange zest

5 oz (155 g) fresh raspberries

5 oz (155 g) fresh strawberries, hulled (stemmed)
and sliced

3 oz (90 g) fresh blueberries

Heat oil in wok or frying pan until it reaches 375°F (190°C) on deep-frying thermometer or until small bread cube dropped in oil sizzles and turns golden. Working in batches, add wonton wrappers and fry until golden on both sides, about 1 minute. Using slotted spoon, remove from pan and drain on paper towels. Allow to cool.

In bowl, combine ricotta cheese, cream, 3 tablespoons of sugar, Grand Marnier and zest. Using electric mixer beat until light and fluffy, 2–3 minutes. Cover and chill until ready to serve.

In another bowl, combine raspberries, strawberries and blueberries. Cover and chill.

To serve, place one wonton on each plate. Spread with ricotta filling. Spoon berries over filling. Top with second wonton. Dust with some of remaining sugar.

Serves 4

CREAM AND BERRY STACK

White chocolate crunch

3 oz (90 g) egg noodles

vegetable oil for deep-frying

10 oz (300 g) white chocolate

1 cup (6 oz/180 g) chopped dried apricots

1/2 cup (2 oz/60 g) sliced (flaked) almonds,
  toasted

Break noodles into smaller pieces. Heat oil in wok or frying pan until it reaches 375°F (190°C) on deep-frying thermometer or until small bread cube dropped in oil sizzles and turns golden. Add noodles and deep-fry until crisp, about 1 minute. Using slotted spoon, remove from pan and drain on paper towels. Allow to cool.

Place chocolate in heatproof bowl. Place over, but not touching, saucepan of simmering water. Stir until chocolate melts. Remove from heat.

Add apricots, almonds and noodles to chocolate. Mix well.

Line baking sheet (tray) with parchment (baking) paper. Place tablespoonfuls of noodle and chocolate mixture on sheet. Refrigerate until firm, 1–2 hours.

Serve crunch chilled. Store in an airtight container in refrigerator.

Makes about 12 pieces

Hints

You may add golden raisins (sultanas) and your choice of nuts to this recipe, if desired.

WHITE CHOCOLATE CRUNCH

Chicken stock

2 lb (1 kg) chicken parts

8 cups (64 fl oz/2 L) water

1 cup (8 fl oz/250 ml) rice wine

4 slices fresh ginger, bruised

Place chicken, water, rice wine and ginger in large saucepan. Bring to boil. Reduce heat to low and simmer, uncovered, for 1½ hours. Skim surface of stock during cooking to remove any foam and discard.

Remove from heat and strain stock through sieve lined with cheesecloth (muslin). Cover and refrigerate until cool, then remove fat from top of stock.

Transfer to airtight containers and refrigerate for up to 4 days or freeze for up to 3 months. Or freeze in ice cube trays, then place in freezer bags.

Makes about 6 cups (48 fl oz/1.5 L)

Fish stock

1 tablespoon vegetable oil

2 cloves garlic, chopped

4 slices fresh ginger, bruised

3 onions, chopped

4 lb (2 kg) fish bones

8 cups (64 fl oz/2 L) water

Heat oil in large saucepan over medium-high heat. Add garlic, ginger and onions and cook until softened, 2–3 minutes. Do not allow to brown.

Add fish bones and water. Bring to boil, reduce heat to low and simmer, uncovered, for 1 1/2 hours. Skim surface of stock during cooking to remove any foam and discard.

Remove from heat and strain through sieve lined with cheesecloth (muslin). Cover and refrigerate until cool, then remove fat from top of stock. Transfer to airtight containers and refrigerate for up to 2 days or freeze for up to 1 month.

Makes about 6 cups (48 fl oz/1.5 L)

Published in 1998 by Periplus Editions (HK) Ltd.,
with editorial offices at 153 Milk Street, Boston, Massachusetts 02109 and
5 Little Road #08-01 Singapore 536983

Library of Congress Cataloging-in-Publication Data is available
ISBN 962-593-459-6

DISTRIBUTED BY

USA
Charles E. Tuttle Co., Inc.
RR1 Box 231-5
North Clarendon, VT 05759
Tel: (802) 773-8930
Fax: (802) 773-6993

Japan
Tuttle Shokai Ltd.
1-21-13, Seki
Tama-ku, Kawasaki-shi
Kanagawa-ken 214, Japan
Tel: (044) 833-0225
Fax: (044) 822-0413

Southeast Asia
Berkeley Books Pte. Ltd.
5 Little Road #08-01
Singapore 53698
Tel: (65) 280-3320
Fax: (65) 280-6290

Set in Frutiger on QuarkXPress
Printed in Singapore

First edition
05 04 03 02 01 00 99   10 9 8 7 6 5 4 3 2